Making Money

---

a how-to book for
a smart girl's guide: money

by Apryl Lundsten
illustrated by Brigette Barrager

Published by American Girl Publishing
Copyright © 2014 American Girl

Questions or comments? Call 1-800-845-0005,
visit **americangirl.com,** or write to Customer Service,
American Girl, 8400 Fairway Place, Middleton, WI 53562-0497.

Printed in China
14 15 16 17 18 19 20 21 LEO 10 9 8 7 6 5 4 3 2 1

All American Girl marks are trademarks of American Girl.

Editorial Development: Darcie Johnston
Art Direction & Design: Sarah Boecher
Production: Tami Kepler, Judith Lary, Paula Moon, Janell Wisecup, Jeannette Bailey

No business of any kind is guaranteed to succeed. Always check with a parent
or guardian before engaging in any of these types of activities.

Dear Reader,

For most of your life, you probably didn't think all that much about money—or how to make it—because Mom and Dad paid for the things you needed. But now that you're older, you may be thinking about earning your own spending (or saving) loot.

Maybe you want to buy a gift for your best friend's birthday or get holiday presents for your family. Maybe you'd like to see a movie with friends. Or maybe you're trying to save up for something bigger, like a new outfit, or a cell phone, or even college. And maybe you'd like to raise dollars to donate to a local animal shelter or help a family in need.

Whatever your reason, this book is full of ideas to help you put change in your purse. From taking care of pets to selling handmade crafts to running a neighborhood car wash, you'll find tons of inspiration—plus the tips and tools to make it all happen.

No matter what business you choose, whether it's in this book or it's your own idea, *Making Money* will help you figure out how to do it. You'll also find ways to make your work easier and more fun; when you see this symbol *play* go to *americangirl.com/play* for printable checklists, marketing materials, and more. This book will even help you discover new things to do with all your hard-earned cash.

So turn the page and get started making money!

Your friends at American Girl

contents

the best biz for you

what's your calling?

There's no limit to the number of ways you can earn money. The key is finding what you're good at and what you like to do—and then figuring out how to turn all that into $$$.

Start by thinking about your strengths and talents. Are you . . .

A born entertainer?

Caring?

Good with math, computers, or electronics?

An organization whiz?

Good with your hands?

Creative?

Comfortable with all kinds of people?

Sporty?

Next, think about what you love to do. What would you do even if you didn't get paid for it? Write down five things:

1. _____

2. _____

3. _____

4. _____

5. _____

Could you turn any of these into a way to make money?

If you like to draw, maybe you could create cards, signs, or portraits of people or their pets.

Or if you're a whiz at organizing, you could help someone redo a closet or clean out her garage.

Maybe you're really good at tech stuff and could teach people some computer basics.

Or maybe you love to be outside, which could make you a great helper for someone with a big yard or a garden.

Some interests are better just as hobbies and might not make a good business. But don't dismiss something you love without imagining all the possibilities first.

is it a moneymaker?

So you know what you love to do, you know your strengths, and you think you might have a good idea. Now ask yourself if people want or need that idea.

Let's say you'd like to make scarves and sell them. Before you get your knitting needles out, consider these things:

Do you live in a cold climate where lots of people need scarves?

Is it winter now?

Have people already asked you to make them one of your amazing scarves?

Are scarves popular right now?

If you answered yes to most of these questions, that's a green light. But if you live in a warm climate, or it's the middle of summer, or people are wearing hats instead of scarves this season, then you'd probably do better if you moved on to your next idea.

Biz quiz

Still not sure? Take this quiz to figure out what might be the right fit for you. Circle the answers that best describe you.

1. Your school is putting on a book fair to raise money, and you're asked to help. You offer to . . .

   a. make bookmarks.

   b. organize the booths and arrange the books.

   c. help line up a band or other type of entertainment.

   d. set up an area or stage and read to kids.

   e. create a special section of books about endangered species.

Quiz

2. Your best friend and you are brainstorming ideas for her upcoming birthday party. You suggest . . .

a. a jewelry-making party.

b. hitting the batting cages or putt-putt golf course.

c. doing your own production of *Cats*.

d. a party where each guest shows the others how to do something she's good at, like a yoga pose, a magic trick, or how to say hello in Swahili.

e. going to the zoo.

3. Your aunt asks you what you want to be when you grow up. You answer . . .

a. an artist, a chef, a writer, a composer—definitely something creative.

b. a mountain guide or landscape architect—or maybe a marine biologist!

c. a dancer, an actress, or some sort of entertainer.

d. a doctor, teacher, lawyer, or social worker—someone who helps people.

e. a veterinarian.

4. You have a whole day to do whatever you want. You're most likely to . . .

a. bake cookies, work on your scrapbook, or make something fun.

b. go swimming, ride your bike, or do some other outdoor activity.

c. practice your pas de bourrée dance moves.

d. join forces with your sister and clean out your closets.

e. take your dog for a walk or play fetch with her.

Answers

Crafty girl

If you answered mostly a's, you're a creative type who feels most comfortable when making things—whether it's cookies, soap, sculptures, or stories. The best kind of business for you would be one that lets you flex your right brain. Consider creating items to sell, such as beaded bracelets or decorative photo frames.

Mover 'n' shaker

If you answered mostly b's, you like to dive in and get things done. You probably don't like sitting still for too long. The type of work that's best for you would be anything where you're active, and maybe outside. Raking leaves or planting flowers, organizing a closet, housecleaning, or running a car wash are good choices. You could even be a sports coach or assistant.

Crowd pleaser

If you answered mostly c's, you're probably super outgoing and love entertaining people. You're likely a performer and might love to dance, sing, or act. Consider dressing up like a clown, magician, or other character and entertaining at birthday parties. Play an instrument or sing? Consider performing at parties or other gatherings. If you're not a performer but like the idea of doing something involving entertainment, you could help organize, create, or run parties for kids.

People person

If you answered mostly d's, you're someone who loves to give back and help others. Tutoring kids who need help in math, reading, or another subject would be perfect, or if you're tech-savvy, you could offer computer training to friends of your parents or grandparents. Another good job for you could be helping an elderly family member or friend with chores and errands. You could also be a parent's helper for moms and dads who need an extra pair of hands (or eyes!) with little ones.

Animal lover

If you answered mostly e's, you probably feel right at home in a pile of puppies. Working with pets would be best for you. Dog walking and pet sitting could make your heart purr!

look around

Still not sure? Maybe try just opening your eyes. There are probably moneymaking opportunities all around you!

Around the house

Are there closets that could be cleaned out?
Drawers to be organized?
A garage to de-clutter?

In the neighborhood

Are there yards that need to be raked?
Snowy driveways or sidewalks to shovel?
Gardens to weed and water?

With people you know

Think about people you know. Maybe some kids on your block need tutoring or would like guitar lessons. Or maybe the family down the street with the new baby needs someone to play with the big sister. Or maybe a neighbor who works all day would like someone to walk her dogs in the afternoon.

Write down the opportunities you see around you:

Around the house

_____

_____

In the neighborhood

_____

_____

With people you know

_____

_____

getting started

ready, set...

You've decided on a great moneymaker. Congratulations! But now what? You've got a few things to think about before you can say GO.

Time

How much time do you have? Be realistic. Will you work after school or only on weekends? Once a week? Once a month?

Supplies

Think about supplies or tools that you'll need. Ingredients? Snow shovel? Gardening gloves? Talk with your parents about how you'll get them and pay for them.

Know-how

What kind of skills does your idea require? Do you need training, or maybe a how-to book?

Practice

Before you open your doors, test out your idea. If your biz is weeding, work on your own lawn or garden first. Or if you're making headbands, create a few samples and wear them to see how they hold up.

Getting the word out

How will people find out about your pet-sitting service or your beautiful bracelets? Maybe you'll want to create a flyer to give to your neighbors and friends. Maybe there's a community newsletter where you can put an ad. Decide with your parents how, where, and to whom you'll market your biz.

Safety matters

No matter what kind of work you're planning, it MUST be safe—for you and your customers. Always check with your parents or another adult before you begin any activity, and always let them know where you're going, what you're doing, and who you'll be with.

Money matters

Set your price
Do some research before you decide how much to charge. Ask what others your age are charging for the same service. Look online with your parents. Check out stores or shops near you.

Count your expenses
You'll probably have **expenses** for supplies or tools. Ink for your printer and paper for flyers. Gardening gloves. Doggy treats and cat toys. When you decide how much to charge, keep your expenses in mind. You don't want to sell your services or items for *less* than what you spent!

Set up a spreadsheet on the computer or make a monthly report form like the one here to help you manage your money. Make a page for every month so that you can see how your biz is doing over time. Record both **income**—how much money you take in—and expenses to get the complete picture.

🐾 Callie's Critter Care 🐾
MONTHLY REPORT: SEPTEMBER

Income

Date	From	Amount
9/1	Loan from Mom to buy supplies	$30.00
9/14	Pet sitting, Beckers' 3 cats, one visit	$10.00
9/16-9/20	Walk Spot and Snail after school	$25.00
9/23-9/27	Walk Spot and Snail after school	$25.00
Total Income This Month:		$90.00

Expenses

Date	For	Amount
9/3	Rawhide bone for Snail	$4.48
9/12	Tote bag for pet-sitting kit	$8.47
9/28	Paid loan (9/1) back to Mom	$30.00
Total Expenses This Month:		$42.95

Profit

$90.00	–	$42.95	=	$47.05
TOTAL INCOME	minus	TOTAL EXPENSES	equals	TOTAL PROFIT

home office

play Keep your biz running smoothly with a filing system for monthly reports and other simple records. Your files can be on the computer (there are programs for this, including some that are especially for kids), or you can use paper and a desk drawer. (See the sample forms at *americangirl.com/play*.)

Monthly reports: for keeping track of your income, expenses, and profit.

Appointment calendar: for keeping track of your appointments. Write them down in this calendar—both dates and times—as soon as you make them.

Client list: for keeping track of your clients' names, phone numbers, addresses, and e-mail addresses. Use this record to write down any notes about clients that you don't want to forget, such as how much you charge them to rake their yard.

Invoices: for keeping track of what clients owe you. If you don't get paid on the spot when you work, create a bill or invoice for the client, and file a copy for yourself so that you don't forget.

Receipts: for keeping track of expenses. Save receipts for things you buy in a folder or envelope.

pairing up

Helper BFFs

Rallying friends can be a great way to work faster and spend time together. Before you sign up your BFF, consider these things:

Paycheck

How much are you going to pay her? Will you split the money 50-50? Will she get a specific amount that you agree on ahead of time?

Work or play?

Having friends work with you can turn work into great fun. It's not a party, though, so make sure anyone who helps is on track to get the job done.

Hard decisions

If a friend is making your work harder, not easier, be honest. Just let her know you don't need her help after all while you get the job done. Try not to let it affect your friendship.

Partnerships

Two can often bring in more business than one. And double the brainpower can add up to double the creative ideas. Here are some things to keep in mind when starting a partnership.

Who does what?

Decide together which of you is responsible for the different things that need to be done. That way neither of you will get confused about who's supposed to handle an important task, and you won't accidentally do the other's job.

It's BETTER TOGETHER

Divide the workload

Splitting tasks helps get the job done faster. Just be sure you know how much time each of you can devote to the business. An equal split is ideal. But sometimes there might be other things going on, like schoolwork or family obligations. Always let each other know when something's coming up that will take you away from the biz.

Split the money

In most partnerships, money is divided evenly. If one partner works more or less than the other, though, the cash should be split according to the amount worked. Also, if one partner has spent money for the biz, then those $$ should be paid back to her out of the pot before you divide the rest.

Write it down

It's best to figure these things out before you hang up your "Open for Business" sign. Write up a partnership agreement that says who's responsible for what and how you'll split the money. (You'll find one at *americangirl.com/play.*)

Talk it out

Communication matters in any relationship—including a business partnership. Share your ideas, goals, and hopes, and talk about fears you might have about your work together. Lay everything out and find solutions as a team.

Friends first

You were friends before you were partners, and you want to stay that way. Take time out to do things that have nothing to do with your business. Watch a movie, ride bikes, or just take a dance break once in a while to keep things light and fun.

customer service

Good customer service can mean more business for you. Satisfied clients will come back for more, and they'll refer you to their friends and family, too. Keep these customer-service points in mind, and you'll have all the biz you can handle!

Time. If you've agreed to meet Mrs. Adams at 9:30 on Saturday morning, arrive at 9:30—or 9:25. If you have to be late, call ASAP and let her know when you can be there.

Attention. Listen carefully to instructions, ask questions, and take notes so that you understand everything and don't forget anything.

Neatness. Pay attention to your appearance, especially the first time you meet. Your client may decide to hire you based on her very first impression.

Attitude. No doubt about it, running a biz can be hard work, but save complaints for your friends and parents. Try to keep your goals in mind, and stay positive with your customers.

Appreciation. Always let your customers know you appreciate their business. Thank them when the project is finished, and follow up with an e-mail or even a handwritten card.

Troubleshooting

Sometimes things come up that you can't help. How would you deal with the following situations?

1. You agreed to rake your neighbor's lawn at 4:30 on Wednesday. On Tuesday you realize you have gymnastics at the same time.

2. You're tutoring a kid in math when you discover you don't know how to do a problem he needs help with.

3. You and your business partner are cleaning a customer's house when you accidentally break something.

4. Your customer tells you that the clasp broke on a bracelet you made.

Stuff happens. Being honest and respectful, doing what you say you'll do, taking charge of finding answers, and telling clients as early as possible about changes and problems are the main ingredients for solving just about any situation. When in doubt, though, ask your mom or dad for help.

Very big tip

Talk to your parents about your moneymaking ideas. Discuss how much time you have for your biz, and how they might help you get started. Ask for their assistance deciding how much to charge, finding people you can work for, and troubleshooting sticky situations. They've been there, and they want you to succeed.

getting the word out

marketing basics

Marketing is a word that describes all the things a biz does to get people's attention. It's how you let people know who you are and what you do.

Coming up with a name and logo for your business

Hanging up posters

Handing out flyers and business cards

Sending e-mails to people you know

Putting ads in your neighborhood newsletter or school paper

Creating a website

Promoting your business with special offers and deals

PURR-FECT PET CARE

Do-it-yourself marketing

play Make your own flyers, business cards, and posters! Go online to *americangirl.com/play,* where you can choose a logo and then design the perfect marketing materials for your budding biz.

what's in a name?

To add pizzazz to your enterprise, give it a great name! Think about companies you know. What do you like about their names? A good name should be easy to remember and tell customers what you do.

Name game

Need a little inspiration for your own business name? Read these names and choose the one that you like most for each biz:

Lemonade stand

- **a.** Stand-Up Lemonade
- **b.** Lemon Crush
- **c.** Pucker Up
- **d.** Lena Loves Lemons

Gardening service

- **a.** Leaf-n-Flower
- **b.** Green Thumb Gardening
- **c.** Yard Scene
- **d.** Clippings Gardening Service

Party planner

- **a.** Party Squad
- **b.** Eve's Excellent Events
- **c.** Happenings Host
- **d.** Celebrate!

Housecleaning

- **a.** Clean Sweep
- **b.** De-grit & De-grime
- **c.** Sparkle-n-Shine
- **d.** House Spiffers

T-shirt painting

- **a.** Arty T's
- **b.** Tee Designs
- **c.** Tee Kart
- **d.** T for U

Logo to go-go

A logo is a picture or design that symbolizes your business. The best ones are simple but memorable. You can use a logo on flyers, ads, business cards, a website—anything that tells people about you.

What kind of business does each of these images make you think of?

a. _____   f. _____

b. _____   g. _____

c. _____   h. _____

d. _____   i. _____

e. _____   j. _____

ways with words

"Hi" flyer

An eye-catching flyer can let clients know what you do and how to reach you.

Mara's Help for Parents

Do you need an extra pair of eyes or another pair of hands?

I can help!

Services: playing with kids inside and out, reading to kids, fixing snacks and lunch, helping with chores

Experience: I have a little brother and baby sister

Summer Hours: any morning or afternoon

References available upon request.
Please call Mara at 555-4567!

Give flyers to friends and neighbors. Post them on a bulletin board at your school, library, or community center. Make a list of names and places with your mom or dad, then have your parent go with you when you deliver them.

Biz cards

A business card is easy to hand out and easy for people to keep on hand. Be creative! Are you working with pets? How about a card in the shape of a bone? Selling hand-painted T-shirts? A card shaped like a shirt is an instant visual!

Walks & Wags
My walks will make your dog's tail wag!

Tabitha
555-9876

What to include in marketing

- Your first name or the name of your biz

- Your service or product

- Your family phone number or family e-mail address

What NOT to include

- Your last name
- Your home address
- Your personal cell phone number
- Your personal e-mail address
- Your photo

more marketing

E-mails

Send an e-mail to your clients with reminders or specials. "Spring is coming! I can spread your mulch before weeds take root!" Or "Fall Special: Buy 2 hours of garage cleaning and get 1 hour FREE!"

Promotions and extras

Add something special so that you stand out. Kick off the gardening season with a packet of flower seeds. If you pet sit, bring a favorite toy. Helping someone clean out a closet? Bring labeled boxes!

house and home

the new homework

Chores. They're a fact of life, no matter how old you are. (Believe it or not, your parents have even more chores than you do!) Every family has different ways of handling them. No matter what, though, you're probably responsible for cleaning your room and a few other things around your home.

You may get an **allowance.** Every family is different when it comes to allowances, too. Often an allowance isn't considered payment for chores. You're just supposed to do those. Instead, it's meant to give you practice with money—and it might stop when you're old enough to make money by working for it.

Being old enough to earn money means:

1. You can have more to spend on what you want and need—and to save and donate to causes you care about.

2. YOU get to decide how you'll earn it!

Supercharged chores! Cleaning your room, emptying the dishwasher, taking out the recycling, walking the dog—your chores are probably regular jobs that help keep daily life running smoothly. But maybe there are extra jobs around the house that your parents would be happy to pay you for—things they have trouble finding time to do, or things they might pay someone else to do. Maybe you could offer to clean the floors every weekend. Or wash the windows. Or clean out the fridge. Or sweep out the garage.

Once you get some practice, you might even be able to do some of these jobs for other people you know, like your grandparents or your next-door neighbors.

house helper

Here are just a few ways to lighten your parents' load around the house while adding weight to your piggy bank.

Pantry-zone purge

Organize the pantry, junk drawer, and other kitchen cupboards. Purge one drawer, cupboard, or shelf each day or weekend. Soon you'll have a neat kitchen, and it won't feel like it took lots of time.

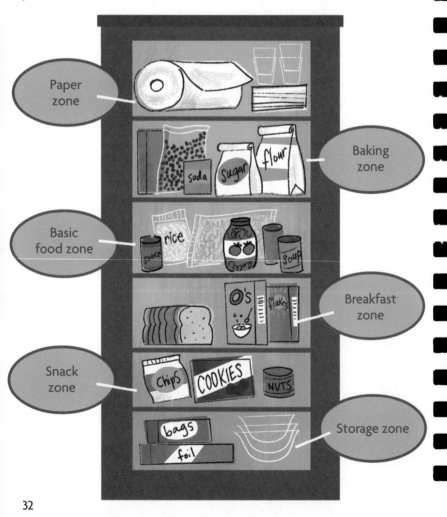

Paper zone

Baking zone

Basic food zone

Breakfast zone

Snack zone

Storage zone

Window wash-up

Let the sun shine in with a spritz and a swipe.

- Make an earth-friendly window cleaner by combining equal amounts of water and distilled white vinegar.

- Spray the glass lightly, and rub until it's completely dry to remove streaks.

- Just use a dry cloth if the windows are clean but a little dusty.

- Newspaper makes a great window-cleaning cloth; use pages that don't have color or lots of black ink.

Tools of the trade
- Spray bottle
- Nontoxic window-cleaning solution
- Lint-free cloth or clean newsprint

Fridge freshening

Clean out and clean up!

- Toss out old food first. Check expiration dates on packages.

- Wipe the shelves and drawers with a soapy sponge. It's easiest to take food out first for this step.

- Placing an open box of baking soda in the fridge will help keep everything fresh when you're done.

Closet clean-out

Make space by putting away the clothes and items you're not using.

- If it's spring or summer, box up winter items. If it's fall, bring out the outerwear, and pack away the warm-weather stuff.

- Dust shelves and sweep or vacuum before hanging clothes back up.

- Donate or recycle items that don't fit or are no longer used or worn. (Check with your parents first!)

Garage sweep

This is a great job to do with your parents—and it can be a fun way to spend time together.

- Get rid of things that are broken, and donate things nobody uses.

- Organize items you're keeping. Create areas and bins for them.

- Move things out of the garage so that you can sweep the floor.

Fun makers

Make the time fly with some creative fun. Hand-write little **love notes** of appreciation, and leave them around the house as you clean for your parents and siblings to find. Put on your favorite tunes and do a little **dust 'n' dance** while you work. **Pretend** you're on a pirate ship scrubbing the galley or you're Cinderella scrubbing the floor before going to the ball.

Scavenger hunt

Write down the following on a piece of paper:

Socks	Mail	DVDs
Shoes	Dishes	Hair accessories
Coats and jackets	Books and magazines	Toys
Backpacks	Remotes	Trash

1. Cut the paper into strips and put them in a bowl.

2. Choose a strip. Then set off to find all of those items in the house and put them in their proper place.

3. Keep doing this until all the strips are gone and the house is completely decluttered.

Money matters

You'll probably get paid by the hour or by the job. Talk to your parents about a price that seems fair to you and to them.

Customer service matters

Customer service is just as important whether you're working for your parents or for another client. Keep Mom and Dad happy, too. They're giving you a big opportunity.

Above and beyond

Remember that you're part of a family. If you see your mom struggling with groceries or you notice the family room is getting messy, pitch in—even if you've already finished your work or chores for the day. Seeing a task that needs to be done and taking the initiative to do it shows you're thoughtful, caring, and mature.

maid parade

If you dust, mop, and sweep in your own house, why not start a business doing these cleaning basics for others? And why not do it with a friend or two? This is a great partnership biz. Your clients can include neighbors, family members, and friends of Mom and Dad.

IT'S BETTER TOGETHER!

Cleaning basics

Each house is different, and families tend to have their favorite cleaning methods. Your clients will provide most of the basics you'll need, including a vacuum, broom, and cleaners they like. You can also ask for things such as rags and a bucket, or bring your own.

Ask which cleaners to use on different surfaces, such as wood, tile, glass, and appliances. Take notes. You might do some research on environmentally friendly cleaners—including ones you can make yourself. They are much better for the planet, your clients, and you!

Dusting

• Remove knickknacks and other items first so that you can be fast and thorough.

• Start at the top and work your way down. Dusting first and cleaning floors last is most efficient.

• Feather dusters look fun and cute, but they don't actually pick up dust—they just move it around. Use a slightly damp cloth instead.

Kitchen

- Wipe counters with a soapy sponge, wipe again with a clean sponge, and then dry with a clean towel.

- On appliances, use either warm soapy water, a spray of vinegar, or a commercial cleaner. Ask your clients what they prefer.

Floors

- Tile and linoleum floors can be swept, then mopped with vinegar water. Just add a cupful of vinegar to a mop bucket of water.

- Sweep and vacuum wood floors, and spot clean with a damp cloth.

- Vacuum carpeting and large rugs. Overlap strokes and change direction a lot to make sure you get everything.

Maid manager

play Make yourself a checklist (or find one at *americangirl.com/play*) to help you remember what to clean and what products to use. You can also leave the checklist with your client to show what you did.

Cleaning Checklist

Kitchen

☐ Clean counters and sink

☐ Clean kitchen appliances

☐ Clean floor

Products used:

Around the House

☐ Empty wastebaskets

☐ Dust

☐ Sweep / vacuum

Products used:

Spot cleaner game

Circle anything you see that needs to be cleaned in this house!

Fun makers

- Play music.
- Turn it into a workout.
- Clean against the clock.
- Give a play-by-play as you clean.
- Whistle (or sing) while you work—it makes it WAY more fun!

Safety matters

Always have a cell phone with you—your own or your parent's.

Open windows for fresh air when you're using cleaners.

Don't answer the door for anyone except Mom, Dad, or the owner of the house.

Don't climb anything that seems unsteady or lift anything too heavy.

Money matters

Decide whether to charge by the hour or by the job. If you charge by the job, first figure out how many rooms you'll be cleaning and exactly what jobs you'll be doing.

Customer service matters

Time it right. Expect the first time or two to take longer while you're getting familiar with the job, and allow enough time. After that, you'll soon be up to speed.

Plan ahead. If you know you can't get all your work done, let your clients know as soon as possible—and have a plan in place for how you'll make it up.

Do your best. Take pride in being the best window washer, dish dryer, or floor mopper ever. Your clients (including your parents) will be happy, and you'll feel good knowing you did a great job.

Clean queen q&a

Q. I broke a vase! It tipped over while I was dusting. What do I do?

A. Let your client know right away, even if you have to leave a note. Apologize and offer to replace the vase. If it's irreplaceable, maybe you could offer a free cleaning service.

Q. I want to listen to music while I clean, but my client is always there. What do I do?

A. You could ask her if it's OK if you listen to music softly. Or bring headphones. That way you can listen to whatever you want and you won't disturb anyone.

Q. My family is going away on vacation, and I'm going to miss my cleaning sessions. What do I do?

A. Reschedule with your clients as soon as you know you'll be away so that they can make other arrangements if they want to.

Q. Whoops! I used the wrong cleaner on the glass coffee table, and now it has streaks. What do I do?

A. There are lots of different cleaning products out there, and each one is used for different surfaces, such as wood, glass, or stainless steel. Ask your client what to use, and read the product label before you use it to find out what it's for. If it looks like you've accidentally used the wrong cleaner, ask an adult to help you figure out how to fix it. Let your client know what happened.

Q. My client asked me to get on a stool and clean the ceiling fan. I'm scared I'm going to fall. What do I do?

A. If you're asked to do anything you're not capable of, it's OK to let her know that while you really want to help out, you don't feel strong enough, prepared enough, or experienced enough to do that task. She should understand.

the great
outdoors

nature girl?

Would you rather . . .

Spring
a. ride your bike or climb a tree
b. write a poem about the budding leaves and blooms

Summer
a. swim in your favorite pool or lake
b. soak in a bubble bath

Fall
a. jump in giant piles of leaves
b. go shopping for school supplies

Winter
a. go skiing or make snow people
b. read and sip hot cocoa in front of the fire

If you chose more a's than
b's, look outside for jobs that
fit your active, nature-loving style.
You'll find opportunities around
every corner, every month of the year.

four-season biz

Every season offers job potential, both at home and around the neighborhood.

Spring: washing outside windows

After months of snow, wind, and rain, windows can use a de-griming to let the spring sun inside.

- Use one teaspoon of dish soap to two gallons of warm water in your bucket.

- Squeeze water out of the sponge, then wipe down the windows.

- Pull the squeegee down the window, and wipe the extra water off the squeegee's edge each time you pull.

- Dry off the drips and the woodwork with a towel.

Summer: watering plants

The summer sun makes gardens thirsty. If Mother Nature doesn't send much rain, the plants will especially love your TLC.

Tools of the trade
• Garden hose
• Shady hat
• Big watering can

- Turn on the water so that a steady but small stream comes from the hose—not too much at a time.

- Water each plant for several minutes so the water goes deep down in the ground. This takes longer, but it makes plants stronger.

- Water in the morning, not when the sun is high in the sky.

- Don't water again until the soil feels dry a couple of inches down.

Pots, boxes, and containers

Plants that live in pots, containers, and window boxes need more watering than plants in the ground because the soil dries out faster.

- Use enough water to get the soil moist all the way through the pot.

- During hot and dry periods, check the pots every day.

Fall: raking leaves

Nothing means autumn more than falling leaves! Rake them up to keep the grass underneath from dying.

- Rake leaves on a sunny day. Wet leaves are hard to pick up.

- Wear gloves to avoid blisters—ouch!

- Be sure to use the right kind of rake. A leaf rake is fan-shaped with flexible tines that scoop up leaves without hurting the grass.

- Rake leaves into many small piles rather than one big one. They're easier to move to the leaf bag or compost bin that way.

Tools of the trade
- Leaf rake
- Gloves

Much ado about mulch

Leaves can stay out of the trash. In many communities, leaves are swept to the curb or put in special bags so that they can be collected and shredded into mulch. Even better: have a compost bin in the backyard, and just dump your leaves into it. The leaves will naturally break down into mulch that can be used the next year or so.

Leaf mulch looks kind of like dirt, but for gardeners it's more like gold. Spread it around a garden in spring, and it helps keep weeds down and plants healthy under the summer sun.

Winter: shoveling snow

Falling snow may mean snowballs and snow angels for kids. But for grown-ups it means driveways and sidewalks that need to be cleared.

Tools of the trade
- Snow shovel
- Sturdy gloves or mittens

- Use a shovel that isn't too big or heavy for you.

- Bend at the knees while you shovel. Any lifting should come from your legs, not your back.

- If you're outside for a while, don't forget water. Even though it's cold, you still need to keep from getting thirsty.

- If you use it, sprinkle salt or sand sparingly.

- Gently stretch your muscles after doing a lot of bending and lifting.

* Hint: Sprinkle sand or a special salt mixture that melts ice on sidewalks and driveways. First, though, talk to your clients—including Mom and Dad. They may not want salt because it can hurt lawns and flowers.

gardener's partner

Do you have (or want) a green thumb? Offer your services to a parent, family member, friend, or neighbor with a garden, and you'll be in business for the season.

Planting primer

Gardeners often buy seedlings or small plants and transplant them from their little containers into the garden. Here's how:

1. Water but don't soak the plants in their containers.

2. Use a trowel to dig a hole where the plant will go.

3. Gently squeeze the bottom of the container while tipping it upside down to release the plant and its soil into your hand.

4. Put the plant and its soil in the hole. The plant's soil mound should be even with the ground where you're putting it.

5. Fill in soil around the plant, and push the soil down.

6. Give the new garden member a drink of water.

* Hint: Plant in the early morning or late afternoon, when the sun is not high in the sky. Your baby plants will do much better.

Wise weeding

How can you tell weeds from other plants? It's easy to see the difference in a lawn, but not so easy in a garden, where there can be lots of different plants. When you're just getting started, ask your client to give you a tour of the garden so that you know what to take care of and what to get rid of!

> ∗ Hint: Water the garden before you weed, and the weeds will be easier to get out.

- Grip the weed close to the ground, and pull up gently but firmly.

- Some weeds can be pulled out easily. But others—such as dandelions—can break off when you give them a tug. Use a trowel or a weeding tool to dig those out completely, down to the roots.

- Pull even the tiniest weeds. By next week they'll be big, so get them now to make your job easier.

- Pulling weeds once a week will help you stay on top of them.

- Wear gloves. Certain weeds are prickly or can irritate your skin.

- The best time to weed is after it rains, when soil is wet and loose enough to let go of the plant roots.

> ∗ Hint: Help adults spread mulch over the soil between plants to keep weeds away. It should be piled loosely (not packed down) at least an inch thick. It should not actually touch the garden plants and shrubs.

Backyard composting

Composting is great for the environment, and it makes your work in the yard and garden easy. A win for the earth, and a win for you!

Yard compost is made of weeds you pull up, raked leaves, grass clippings, old flowers—any part of a plant that you remove from the garden or lawn. In the compost, it all breaks down and turns into mulch or soil that you can use in the garden or pots.

Gardeners can buy a compost bin, build a simple one themselves, or just make a space in the back corner of the yard for a compost pile. A compost pile won't turn to mulch or soil as fast as compost in a bin will, but it's just as good for the environment.

- Put only yard plants—no food—in the compost. This will help keep animals from visiting.

- Think green and brown. Green plants and grass clippings plus brown leaves and pruned branches make great compost.

- Offer to rake the lawn after it's mowed, and put all the grass clippings in the bin or pile instead of in lawn bags.

- In the fall, raked leaves also go in the compost instead of in more bags. Soooo easy!

Safety matters

Wear a sunhat and sunblock with an SPF of at least 30.

Avoid gardening in the middle of the day when the sun is hot.

Keep a water bottle with you.

Work with your parent or client nearby.

Money matters

play If you're working regularly for a client, use a notebook to keep track of your time, and have your customer sign it when you work. Then each week just add up the amount you earned, and make a copy of the page from your notebook to give her. (Go online to *americangirl.com/play* for a sample timesheet like the one here.)

Gardener's Partner Timesheet
Week of July 10

Date	Time Started	Time Done	Time Worked	What We Did	Sig
7/10	9:15	11:00	1 hr, 45 min	Planted sunflowers	GAJ
7/12	3:30	4:30	1 hr	Watering	GAJ
7/13	9:00	10:30	1.5 hrs	Weed veg garden & flowers	GAJ
7/16	4:30	5:15	45 min	Watering	GAJ

TOTAL HOURS WORKED: 5 hours x $7.50 = $37.50

Above and beyond

Hmm. You've noticed there are lots of gardening services in your neighborhood. How do you distinguish your biz from those?

Go organic

Teach yourself about pesticides, fertilizers, and other things gardeners might use to make plants grow and keep bugs away. Find out which products are not toxic to the earth, children, and animals. Then talk with your clients. They'll probably be glad to benefit from your knowledge, and the garden will be happy, too.

Parsley Oregano Basil Catnip

Work with kids

Teach your clients' young children about gardening. This could be a fun way to get some help, too!

Edible garden

Offer to create a beautiful and yummy herb garden in a pot to set by the kitchen door.

Hint: Give your clients a couple of recipes that call for your fresh herbs!

1. Buy three to five herb seedlings, such as oregano, thyme, parsley, dill, basil, or chives. Try to vary the colors and shapes of the herbs to make your garden pretty.

2. Fill a large garden pot with potting soil or good garden dirt.

3. Plant the seedlings around the pot, evenly spaced. The herbs will grow, so plant them about 8 inches apart so they have room.

4. Water the soil. Be gentle. A heavy stream of water will flatten small plants.

car-wash whiz

Consider offering a car wash every Saturday to neighbors, relatives, and family friends. This is another great business to do with one or more partners.

Tools of the trade

Car soap

A step stool to reach the roof

Soft cloth towels for drying

Sponge just for wheels

Plushy sponge, or a sponge mitt made from sheepskin or microfiber

Hose

Bucket

How to wash a car

Get ready

1. Set up your biz in the shade. The sun will cause water to leave spots on the car.

2. Fill your bucket with water and car soap, using a fresh bucket for each car. Use soap made specifically for washing cars—dish soap is hard on the car's wax coating.

3. Have a hose ready for rinsing before and after washing.

4. Make sure the car's windows are all closed!

Get to it

1. Rinse the car with clean water from the hose.

2. Wash the car with the soft sponge and soapy water, starting at the top (the roof) and moving down.

3. As each section is done (roof, sides, hood), rinse it with the hose. To conserve water, turn off the hose when you're not using it. When washing with a partner, one of you can be in charge of the hose. Or you can use a separate sponge and bucket of clean water for rinsing to conserve even more.

4. Scrub the wheels (not the tires) with the wheel sponge. Rinse.

5. Use towels to dry, starting with the windows and mirrors. Wipe down the body of the car. Microfiber towels absorb more water and make drying time much faster.

6. Wipe the door jambs, and open the trunk to dry the edges.

7. Dry the windshield wiper blades.

Safety matters

Wear sunscreen and a hat. Water might keep you cool, but the sun is just as strong even when you don't feel it.

Always have a parent or another adult present, especially if your customers are paying with cash at the car wash.

Money matters

Keep the money you collect in a safe location, out of sight and supervised by an adult.

Consider putting out a clear tip jar. Place a couple of one-dollar bills in the jar, and label it "Tips."

Marketing matters

Give flyers advertising your car wash to neighbors. Be sure to include your location and the day and time when you're open for business.

Create a sign to put out at the car wash on washing day. Make one with stiff poster board, or prop up a large chalkboard on the ground or an easel.

Give coupons to your customers offering them a free wash after you've washed their car a certain number of times—you decide how many times before the free one.

what would you do?

1. Your neighbor asks you—for the tenth time (you've been counting)—to make sure you water the herb pot by the back door. You . . .

   a. roll your eyes and say, "Yeah, I KNOW!"

   b. smile and thank her for reminding you.

2. The last time you were planting pansies at the Lee house, you accidentally left the trowel in the garden. Mr. Lee mentions that he found it and put it in the garage. You . . .

   a. say that someone else must have used it after you.

   b. apologize, let him know it won't happen again, and offer to replace it if it was damaged.

3. Your new neighbor Mrs. Yep calls to ask if you can take care of raking her leaves this fall like you do the Solange family's. You . . .

   a. say you're tired of doing that, but thanks anyway.

   b. tell her you'd be happy to meet with her and talk about raking and any other yard work needs she might have. When you get off the phone, you call the Solanges and thank them for telling Mrs. Yep about you.

4. You just finished washing Mr. Cantor's minivan when he points out a spot you missed. You worked really hard on his car and are pretty sure you didn't miss a spot. You . . .

   a. tell him next time he can wash his own car.

   b. scrub the spot again until he's satisfied. After all, the customer is always right.

(If you answered all b's, you get an A+ in customer service!)

pet projects

animal lover?

- Does your head turn whenever you see a cute dog? (And let's face it, every dog is cute!)

- Do you pride yourself on knowing just how a cat likes to be stroked between its shoulder blades?

- Do you know all the healthy things a rabbit likes to eat?

- Do you like to imitate the sounds of the dogs, cats, birds, and other animals you know?

- Do you have pictures of puppies, kittens, and other baby animals on your walls?

- Do you know the names of all your neighborhood's pets?

- Do you love to gaze at colorful fish swimming in their aquarium?

- Do you wish you had more pets than you already have?

- Do you think you might be a vet some day?

If you answered yes to some (or all!) of these questions, then a biz that gets you up close and personal with furry, feathered, and fishy friends might be purrrr-fect for you!

dog walker

Dogs are everywhere! And dogs need walking—for fun, for exercise, and to take care of their own business. Walking a dog or two in your neighborhood is an ideal after-school job. You get fun time outside, and you still have time for homework.

Tools of the trade
- Water
- Water dish
- Extra leash
- Toys
- Treats
- Waste bags
- Emergency numbers

✳ Hint: Interview the owner before you walk her dog the first time. (You'll find an interview form at *americangirl.com/play.*) Things will go better if you know what to expect.

play

Interview questions

What are Fido's favorite routes?

Does Rover like other dogs?

What does Spot like to do on a walk?

Is Scout friendly with people?

What is Lucy's age and breed?

Are there things and places to avoid?

What are Snoopy's favorite playthings?

What time of day does Mimi usually walk?

Are treats okay?

What's the best number if I need to call you?

Pick-up pro

Take at least two plastic waste bags on a walk to pick up any dog droppings. Use the bag like a glove to pick up droppings and keep your hands clean. Tie bags and place them in trash bins.

- Meet the dog and go on a practice walk before you agree to the job.

- Don't walk more dogs than you can handle at the same time.

- Always use a leash, and carry an extra one with you.

- Know the dog's commands and use them. Sit! Stay!

- Follow your community's rules about dogs.

- Stop for a drink break if it's warm outside or your walk is longer than 30 minutes. Bring a bowl and enough water for both of you.

- Always carry spare waste bags and pick up after the pup.

Out and about

Dogs love to sniff! It's one of the most fun things for them, so let your pup smell the roses—and more—along the way. If you can, change up the streets and parks you visit; new sights and smells are a great doggy treat.

Be a true pooch pal. Talk and sing about what you're both seeing, hearing, and smelling. Your dog may talk and sing back!

If it's safe and your dog is able, break into a run from time to time.

Take a drink 'n' pet break under a favorite tree.

Money matters

Ask dog-walking friends what they charge to get an idea of the going rate.

It's best to start at the lowest price until you get more experience—and more customers.

Charge by the walk or the day, or even by the week or month if you walk a dog regularly, such as every day after school.

Safety matters

Walk only where your parents have said it's OK to walk.

Choose streets and parks where lots of people are outside. Stay away from areas that are deserted.

Keep on the sidewalk, cross streets at crosswalks and corners, and obey all signs.

Don't wear earphones. Be alert to what's happening around you.

critter sitter

Pet sitting means a lot of responsibility—and a lot of reward. Your animals are depending on you to take care of them, and they will be grateful for the love and attention they get from you.

Your job is to stop by the pets' home one or two times a day to . . .

Make sure water dishes are filled.

Give them love and attention.

Feed them.

PLAY!

Keep pet areas clean.

Walk dogs.

Before

Before you agree to pet sit, set up a meeting with the owner and her pet. Talk about what is expected of you, the pet's needs and personality, and what you charge per visit or per day.

Meet the pet! You need to know if you're comfortable taking care of the animal, and it needs to get to know you, too.

Don't sit if you're afraid of the pet. It won't be a good situation for either one of you.

Make sure the pet's owner shows you where all the supplies are and how to do tasks like scooping litter or feeding the fish.

play Call or visit a day or two before your job begins. Have a pet-sitting checklist like the one on the next page (get it online at *americangirl.com/play*), and go over it with the pet's owner.

Pet-Sitting Checklist

Date and Time of Departure: _____

Date and Time of Return: _____

Owner's Cell Phone: _____

Destination and Phone Number: _____

Emergency Contact: _____

Vet Information: _____
_____

Type of Food and Amount: _____
_____

Feeding Schedule: _____
_____

Water Bowls: _____

Walks: _____
_____
_____
_____

Other Info:

During

The owner has put the care of her pet in your hands. Don't give the reins to anyone else, unless you've already cleared it with the owner.

Call the owner or your parent immediately if something seems to be wrong with the pet.

Leave your own pet at home or outside, away from the pets you're caring for, unless they have a history of hanging out together.

To be sure you don't miss any instructions, have the pet-sitting checklist with you every time you visit.

Don't give the animals more food than they're supposed to get, even if they do cute things to try to persuade you.

Treat animals as if they're your own pets. Take time to cuddle and play with them. They miss their people and are very happy to see you!

Clean up any mess left by the pet.

Plan to spend 30 to 45 minutes per visit.

Be sure to lock doors and windows when you leave.

After

Check in with the owner as soon as you think she's home to **make sure she's really back.** If she was unexpectedly delayed and not able to reach you, the pets are not being cared for!

3 things about...

Dogs

1. Find out what kind of treats the dog is allowed, and bring a few.

2. Unless you know the pup well, let him sniff you out and get comfortable with you before you bend down and pet him.

3. Pooches love to be spoken to and often respond with head tilting or even barks. Ask the dog about her day. Tell her about yours. It may feel silly, but it's a great way to give attention.

Cats

1. Cats are often shy and may disappear when you arrive. Don't take it personally. He'll come out once he feels comfortable, especially if you're calm and quiet.

2. Most cats love to play. A catnip toy or even a small wadded-up ball of paper can be loads of fun.

3. Cats should not drink milk. It's bad for their digestion.

Fish

1. Goldfish can tell the difference between shapes, colors, and sounds! Try placing photos around their tank.

2. Make sure the temperature in and around a fish tank is not too warm or too cold.

3. Never add water to a fish tank without talking to the owner first.

Safety matters

Keep your pet-sitting checklist with you.

Pet sit only during the day.

Lock the door while you're in the house.

Keep a cell phone with you, or know where the house phone is.

Talk with your parent and the owner about bringing a friend or family member with you.

If you think something may be wrong with the animal or the home, call your parents or the owner right away—even if you're not sure.

Don't tease a pet when it's eating.

Let a sleeping pet sleep. Startling it could cause aggression.

Always keep dogs on leashes when walking them.

Don't approach animals you don't know.

Money matters

For pet sitting, you can charge by the visit, the day, or the week.

Zadie's Critter Sitter Rates

Per visit: $8
Per day (two visits): $12
Per week: $50

Marketing matters

Tell friends and neighbors about your pet services with a cute flyer.

Purrfect Pet Sitting

Do you work long hours? Are you going on vacation?

**I can help make sure your pet is happy
and healthy while you're away.**

Services: feeding, dog walking, cleanup, playing,
oodles of cuddles

About Me: I've been a dog and cat owner for five years
and have lots of experience caring for them.
I love animals and someday want to be a vet.

References: Andrea and Doug Wilson, 916-555-1212
Teri Rhodes, 703-555-1212

Call me today! 818-555-1212

Fill baggies with dog treats, and attach your business name and contact info.

Fit a business card in the lid of a metal mint tin, place a magnet on the card, and give a biz card lid to your clients. They can put it up on their fridge or magnetic board and always have your info handy.

Customer service matters

Be there
When taking care of pets, it's soooo important that you show up on time. Animals don't have a voice, and they can't get their own food and water. They are counting on you to take care of them!

Be thorough
Pet owners want what's best for their pets, and they're relying on you to make sure that happens. Be sure to do everything they ask.

Be present

When taking care of critters, put your heart and mind into it. They will sense that you care and look forward to your visits. Sure, they're excited about dinner, but they also love it when you play, cuddle, and talk. See that tail wag!

Be communicative

When the owner is back, tell her stories about her pet, the little things you noticed, and what you did together.

Above and beyond

Offer to gather mail, bring in the newspaper, and water plants.

Take and send photos or videos of the pet to the owner. This will make the owner feel connected to her pet even while she's away.

Keep a daily diary describing what the pet did. Include playtime, cuddles, feeding, and walking. Make it fun by writing the entries from the pet's point of view!

10/29 Wed. 3:30 p.m.
Girl came through door! HOORAY!!!
Loved catnip mouse she brought. Big fat one.
Good kibble too. Yum. Fresh water. Slurp
slurp. Curled up on her lap for after-dinner
nap. She's good at scratching my neck where
I can't reach. Purrrr. Miss you, Mom, but
I like Girl just fine. I don't even hide from
her anymore.
Love,
Coco

helping
hands

what do you know?

In your family and around your neighborhood, there are people who could probably use your know-how.

Maybe you have amazing party ideas to share.

Maybe your grandmother could use some help with errands.

Maybe you're really good with little kids.

These are just some of the ways you can use your skills, ingenuity, and helping hands to start your own biz!

safety checklist

play Before you do any job that involves working with people, make sure both you and your parents can answer yes to every question in this safety checklist (also available at *americangirl.com/play*):

- ☐ I know and trust the person I'm working for. Or Mom and Dad know and trust the person I'm working for.
- ☐ I will call Mom or Dad when I arrive and again when I leave the job site.
- ☐ I will always have a fully charged cell phone with me.
- ☐ I have phone numbers on me in case of an emergency.
- ☐ I don't approach strange animals I don't know.
- ☐ When I am in a house alone, I will lock the door, and I will not answer if someone knocks or rings the bell.
- ☐ When working with people I don't know well, I will take along a parent, another adult, or a friend until my parents say I can go by myself.
- ☐ Mom and Dad will meet anyone I am going to work with.
- ☐ If house or pet sitting, I will not go to a house after dark.
- ☐ I will not use a stove or other appliance.
- ☐ I know how to reset a smoke alarm.
- ☐ I will tell Mom and Dad or another adult if a situation makes me uncomfortable.

parent's helper

A parent's helper watches and plays with kids while their parent is at home. Helpers make it possible for moms and dads to get other things done around the house, take care of a new baby, or even just get some rest. Bonus: Being a parent's helper is a great way to get the experience to become a babysitter.

Two-way interview

play You'll want to interview the parents before taking a job, and they'll want to learn more about you, too. Tell them about your experience. Discuss when you can work and how much you charge. And learn about the kids! (A sample interview form is at *americangirl.com/play.*)

Babysitting?

Babysitting requires a whole book's worth of know-how. If you're ready for it, check out *A Smart Girl's Guide: Babysitting* and *Super Sitter's Playbook*, both from American Girl.

Interview questions

What are Brixton's favorite things to eat and drink?

What are your rules about foods and snacks?

Does Kendra have any allergies?

Is it OK if we use the computer?

What are Emma's favorite things to do?

Is Jaden allowed to watch TV or videos?

Where can we play outside?

Carry a backpack with books and toys that are just right for the age of the child, and change what you bring each time. Check out picture books from the library, or bring your old favorites. Balls and simple toys that let you use your imagination are usually the most fun. Always check with parents to make sure any toys are safe before you play with them.

Tools of the trade
• Picture books
• Music CDs
• Games and toys

• Try to give kids either/or choices such as, "Do you want to play ball or read a book?" and "Would you rather have a banana or a pear?"

• Gently distract them with other activities when they're upset.

• Being funny is a great way to help kids get over feeling frustrated, sad, or cranky.

• Listen and talk with them—they are real people!

• Kids love music and rhythm. Singing or playing music together can instantly turn a frown into a smile.

• Playing pretend games with blocks, dolls and stuffed animals, trains and trucks, dress-up clothes, and other parent-approved items can keep kids happy for long periods of time.

7 things to do on a rainy day

1. Make a city with blocks, boxes, plastic bowls and tubs, and toys. Include a train station, a school, your house—let your imaginations run wild.

2. Set up goals around the room and roll balls into them. Score!

3. Dress up and pretend you're royalty, animals in the jungle, or pirates. Use character voices—*Arrr, matey!*

4. Play children's CDs. Dance and sing to the music, and act out any of the words. The sillier, the better.

5. Cuddle up in a cozy place with a stack of picture books. Books are a window on the world for kids. Read old favorites and new stories, too.

6. Make a delicious parent-approved snack to share.

7. Play "I Spy," a matching game, or hide-and-seek. Play all three!

Winding down

Before you go, pick up after yourself and the kids. Get them to help, too. Make it a game by seeing how fast you can put things away or by singing or doing something silly. If there's a lot to do, tackle one task at a time—first the blocks, then the dress-up clothes, then the books, then the toy dishes . . .

Safety matters

Theirs. Safety matters more than ever when you're taking care of little people. The parents will talk with you about safety around stairs, the kitchen, water, doors and windows, bookcases, electrical cords and outlets, small things that are choking hazards, and more. Here are two general rules to always keep in mind:

> **1.** Never leave a child alone, not even for a few seconds.
> **2.** Never leave the house or try something new without checking with the parents.

Yours. Your safety matters just as much. Follow the parents' rules for your own sake, too.

Money matters

A parent's helper is usually paid by the hour. Check with others to find out what they're charging. If this is your first time, you might charge less while you're learning, then negotiate a little more after a few months.

Customer service matters

Parents want to know that their children are **SAFE.** Always follow the rules, ask questions if you're not sure, and get help when you need it.

Parents want to know that their children are **HAPPY.** Be creative, get to know and understand the kids, and have fun with them.

elder's helper

The word "elder" means more than "older." It also means an older person who is respected for wisdom or experience *because* of being older.

An elder's helper is someone who helps an older person with things that may be getting hard for them because of their age. Maybe a grandparent or another older person in your family or neighborhood could use a little help once or twice a week.

Things you can do

Put away groceries

Water plants

Make lunch or snacks

Take out trash and recycling

Dust, sweep, and do other light housekeeping jobs

Wash and put away dishes

Fold laundry

You can also help by keeping a list of items that your elder needs, such as dish soap or lightbulbs, and another list of things that need to be fixed or replaced. Your elder can shop, make calls, or give these lists to an adult helper.

Consider this

Imagine what life was like when your elder was your own age. Think about historical events you've learned about in school—when your elder might have been a child or a young adult. Think how machines and technology have changed. Your elder probably has many wonderful stories to tell!

Bonus: If your elder is a grandparent or another close family member, working for her gives you a special chance to discover your family's history. Ask her to help you fill out your family tree.

Looking back

Your elder might enjoy answering these questions for you:

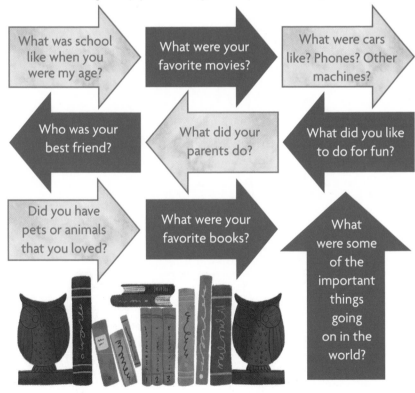

What was school like when you were my age?

What were your favorite movies?

What were cars like? Phones? Other machines?

Who was your best friend?

What did your parents do?

What did you like to do for fun?

Did you have pets or animals that you loved?

What were your favorite books?

What were some of the important things going on in the world?

You could also interview your elder and record your conversations or write them down. You could then make a CD or scrapbook to give to your elder and the family.

Safety matters

If your elder falls, is injured, or seems ill, call your parents or another adult for help. The elder's doctor info, emergency numbers, and relatives' phone numbers should be handy.

If it seems serious—even if you're not sure—call 911.

Money matters

If your elder is a family member, you'll probably want to charge a special price. Part of the benefit for you is being able to spend time with her. Talk with your parents. You may be helping them, too, by helping your elder. Together you can decide on an amount that is best for everyone.

Customer service matters

5 qualities of a GREAT elder's helper

Dependability
Respect Cheerfulness
Trustworthiness
Compassion

party person

Are you a natural host? Helping parents plan or pull off parties for their kids could be the ticket for you, especially if you're good at any of these party essentials:

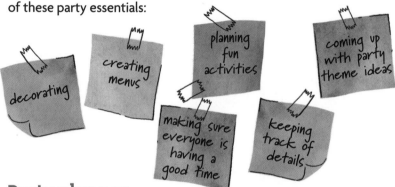

decorating

creating menus

planning fun activities

coming up with party theme ideas

making sure everyone is having a good time

keeping track of details

Party planner

Are themes your thing? Do you have a flair for food or delight in decorating? Planning a party includes many creative jobs:

Make or fill out invitations, and address them.

Create decorations that go with the party theme— and put them up.

Plan and prepare yummy food and drinks.

Be at the party to make sure everything runs smoothly!

Dream up fun games and entertainment.

Enchanting entertainer

Do you love the limelight? Are you an actress? Do you sing or play an instrument or have another unique talent? Even if you don't help plan the party, you can be a focus of fun.

Be a character. Dress up as a princess or queen, fairy godmother, dinosaur, favorite animal, or any other character that fits the party theme. Speak in character. Bring simple props, such as a crown or wand.

Mystify with magic tricks. Wear your cloak, bring your hat, and amaze everyone with feats of magic and card tricks.

Make music. Prepare a playlist of theme songs and deejay the party. Or bring your guitar and lead kids in favorite songs.

Draw on demand. Set up your easel and dash off impressions of each child, or draw theme-related pictures by request.

Conduct a party train. Create a train ride, with you in the lead role of conductor. Get all of your passengers on board behind you, and take them along a route that you've planned, indoors and out, with scenes and obstacles along the way. All aboard!

Safety matters

At the party, make sure the client or other parents are present and looking out for the safety of all the children.

Money matters

You can charge by the hour, in which case you'll need to keep track of your time. Or you and your client can agree on an amount that covers everything. Or you could ask one amount for planning help, and another amount for helping or entertaining during the party.

play Work out an agreement with your client like the one on the next page. Include what you'll be doing, how much you're charging, and when you'll be paid. Write it down, and give a copy to the client as soon as you start working. (You can find an agreement form at *americangirl.com/play*.)

Sara's Super Soirees

Date: April 18

Client: Jennifer Williams, 6092–A Carolinda Ct.

Party details: A birthday party for Kylie Williams from 11 to 1 at the Williams house

Guests: Ten 4-year-olds

Services provided: Sara will address invitations, arrive an hour before party time, and put up decorations. The party has a cat theme. Sara will assist at the party. Sara will lead a game of "Pin the Tail on the Cat" and a "Meow Chorus." Sara will serve food and clean up after the party.

Services not provided: Client will provide decorations, cat cake, paper goods, party favors, and all food and drinks. Client will be supervising the party.

Fee: $25. Please pay at the end of the party.

I agree to these terms: *Jennifer Williams*
Sara

Marketing matters

Ask your clients if they'd be willing to write a recommendation for you. You can show letters to new clients, or include the comments on a flyer or ad with their permission.

"Sara was terrific. She has creative ideas, she's a lot of fun, and the kids loved her. I'd hire her for all my parties!"

"Sara made my son's birthday the best one ever— his words. She came up with tons of fun themes to choose from. Eventually we want to do them all! Thanks, Sara!"

Customer service matters

Be creative. Make things fresh. Your attitude will make people want to hire you. Plus, it'll make things more fun for you!

sale away

look the other way?

Basically, there are **two ways to make money:** selling a service and selling a product. Cleaning houses, caring for children and pets, and shoveling snow are great service businesses. But maybe they aren't for you.

Do any of these describe you—or give you ideas?

Your first moneymaker was a lemonade stand.

You can't bear to just get rid of your old toys and books. SOMEBODY could use them!

Your friends love the bead bracelets you make, so you've started making jewelry for them, too.

If so, instead of offering a service, you might want to sell something.

Crafts or accessories that you make
- Things you knit, such as scarves and headbands
- Things you sew, such as doll clothes
- Things you make with paper and art supplies, such as greeting cards

Food and drinks
- Cookies and caramel corn
- Hot chocolate with marshmallows
- Lemonade!

Your own gently used but outgrown items
- Dolls and accessories
- Picture books
- Toys
- Sports gear

setting up shop

Deciding where and how to sell your product is as important as deciding *what* to sell. Sometimes the where and how will even help you decide the what. A house party is ideal for accessories that you make or sew. A bake sale is perfect for—what else?—your favorite cookies, brownies, or cupcakes.

House party

Have a party where your items are displayed so that people can see and buy them. Invite your friends and their parents, neighbors, and friends of your parents. Offer refreshments and play music.

Outdoor stand

If you live someplace where lots of people walk by your house, set up a stand in your yard with items that suit the season or an event— warm scarves or cool ankle bracelets, holiday crafts, hot or cold drinks and snacks. Decorate your stand and make signs.

Door-to-door

Neighbors can be the best customers for your handmade wares, crafts, baked goods—anything made personally by you. Just make sure Mom and Dad are with you when you're selling or delivering.

Craft fair or bake sale

Reserve a booth at a school fundraiser, church bazaar, or community craft fair, and create a dashing display.

- Group similar items or colors together.

- Think of clever ways to show off your wares.

- Spread your items out so that everything is visible.

- Create cute, informative signs.

- Talk to people about what makes your item special. Do you use only organic ingredients? Are your T-shirts 100 percent cotton? Do you make your own paper for your cards?

Online sales

A good way to sell your used toys and books is through a website. Take photos of your sale items, and write an ad. Then have your parents—not you—post the ad and answer customer e-mails.

Ad tips
- Say exactly what the item is.
- Be honest about its condition.
- Describe any special features.
- Name your price.
- Include your parents' e-mail address.

Photo tips
- Use good lighting.
- Shoot the item against a plain wall or a plain sheet backdrop.
- Take more than one picture, such as close-ups of important details or views of the front, back, and sides.

Pricing tips
- Expect people to bargain!
- When customers ask your parents to lower the price, your parents can talk with you first and then negotiate on your behalf.

Safety matters

- Always have a parent or another adult with you when selling, whether at a lemonade stand in your driveway, a bake-sale booth, or a house party, or going door-to-door.

- Store money in a safe place, out of sight. Keep only a small amount of change on hand, and take your earnings inside from time to time or give them to a parent to keep safe.

- Include only your first name and a family phone number or family e-mail address—not your own—on business cards or flyers that you give to your customers. Never correspond with anyone on your own.

Money matters

Decide your price

If you're selling new items you've made or things to eat or drink, your price should be based on your expenses and—like other businesses—the going rate of similar items.

- Figure out what it costs to make one of your bracelets, cupcakes, scarves, or doll hats. Add up the cost of all the materials you used to make it.

- Whatever the total cost of the materials, double it to get the minimum price you should ask.

- Your prices should be fair for everyone, including you. If you ask too much, no one will buy your stuff. But if you charge too little, you won't make any money.

Make change

Have plenty of change so you don't have to turn customers away. Start with 20 one-dollar bills and lots of coins.

If your parents give you the money for your change box, pay them back after the sale out of your earnings.

Try to price items so that you can make change easily. Ask $1 instead of 99 cents or $1.25. Offer "5 for a dollar" instead of 20 cents apiece to sell more and so that making change is easier.

Practice challenge!

Pretend you sold a bracelet for $3.18 (which you wouldn't really do, but this is an example), and the customer paid you with a $10 bill. Your challenge: Figure how much change to give her. Starting with the price of the item, count up to the amount she gave you. Count out loud as you place the coins and bills down:

START: $3.18

+ 🪙 = $3.19   + 🪙 = $3.20

+ 🪙 = $3.25

+ 🪙 = $3.50   + 🪙 = $3.75   + 🪙 = $4.00

+ 💵 = $5.00

+ 💵 = $10.00

Now you try it, using different starting amounts.

Offer a receipt

Keep blank receipts on hand and fill one out if a customer asks for it.

- Business name
- Date
- What she bought
- How many she bought
- How much she paid

RECEIPT	**Jane's Silky Scarves**
	October 5
	Description:
	1 blue striped scarf $10
	1 orange wool ruffle scarf $12
	Total: $22

Marketing matters

- Use colorful paint or permanent marker or symbols to make your signs stand out.

- Make sure words are clear and easy to read. Use a light background and dark letters at least a few inches tall.

- Use a sturdy material, such as poster board or cardboard, so that signs won't bend in the wind.

Customer service matters

- Treat everyone as if they're your best customer.

- Try to avoid phone calls or texts while customers are visiting your booth.

- Check the items being bought to make sure they're in perfect condition.

- Give the right change. Double-check to make sure you get it right. Triple-check if you need to.

- Say thanks, and let customers know you'd love to see them again.

50
great things to do with your money

Save it

1. Keep $ in your sock drawer for emergencies.
2. Open a savings account.
3. Put $ aside each month toward college.
4. Each week put $1 in a piggy bank that you can't open unless you break it.
5. Plan ahead so that you have plenty of moola for holiday gifts.
6. Your family is going on a road trip next summer, so save for spending cash.
7. Put part of your paycheck toward Space Camp.
8. Keep a chunk for the pure satisfaction of saving.

Spend it wisely

9. Ask yourself if you really need it.
10. Ask yourself if you'll really wear it.
11. Ask yourself how many times you'll wear it.
12. Ask yourself if it fits.
13. Ask yourself how long it will last.
14. Wait for it to go on sale.
15. Use coupons or discounts.
16. Look for used items online.
17. Go to thrift stores and consignment shops.
18. Buy last year's edition or the floor model.

Learn about it

19. Read a good book about money.
20. Know how to read a bank statement.
21. Ask your parents' banker how a savings account works.
22. Learn how a checking account works.
23. Balance a checkbook.
24. Find out how a credit card works.
25. Find out how a debit card works.
    (It's really different from a credit card.)
26. Find a website for teens about money, and visit the site at least once a week.

Give it back

27. Send $20 to help families in need after a hurricane or earthquake.
28. Give one tenth of your earnings to help girls go to school in Africa.
29. Contribute $5 to a local animal shelter.
30. Buy books for your school's auction.
31. Buy a bookstore gift card for your teacher.
32. Pick a charity that means a lot to you, and pledge an amount every month.

33. Donate your money and time to help preserve a wildlife habitat.

34. Give $1 to a food pantry every month—it can provide several meals!

35. Pay for and make posters to announce a cleanup day for a park.

36. Contribute to your school's fundraisers.

37. Ask your grandparents to give money to your favorite cause for your birthday.

38. Donate 25 percent of your bake-sale earnings to a homeless shelter.

39. Sell your books and give the money to your library.

40. Purchase new toys for a family in need during the holidays.

Do something for someone

41. Buy Mom a birthday present.

42. Bring Grandma a bouquet of her favorite flowers—just because.

43. Buy your dad his favorite milkshake.

44. Send your best friend the latest single from her favorite band.

45. Treat your cousin to a movie.

46. Get your sister the new book in her favorite series.

47. Surprise your family by ordering a pizza for dinner.

48. Get your dog a new chew toy.

49. Get your brother new strings for his guitar.

50. Bring the librarian at your school a basket of treats.

Do you have moneymaking experiences or advice to share? Tell us!

Write to: *Making Money* Editor
American Girl
8400 Fairway Place
Middleton, WI 53562.

Here are some other American Girl books you might like.

Discover online games, quizzes, activities,
and more at **americangirl.com/play**